Tbilisi Loves You
42 Poems

Brant von Goble

Loosey Goosey Press
Okemos, Michigan

Loosey Goosey Press
2222 W. Grand River Ave
Okemos, MI 48864

Copyright © 2021 Brant von Goble
(ISNI: 0000 0004 6433 5918)
License: CC Attribution-NonCommercial 4.0 International
(https://creativecommons.org/licenses/by-nc/4.0/)

ISBN: 979-8-9853386-3-8 (Hardcover)
ISBN: 979-8-9853386-8-3 (eBook)
LCCN: 2021951445

Contents

Introduction	vii
Abandon	1
Ad Hoc/Tethers	2
Bondage/Neuroleptic	3
Coercion	4
Context	5
Damming	6
Decadence	7
Demon Core	8
Disconnect	9
Extra!	10
Fatigue	11
Film/Barriers	12
Flavors	13
Genius	14
Hitchcock	15
Kanagawa	16
Legs	17
Lingua Franca	18
Magnanimity/Unusual	19
Nausea	20
Optic/Fiber/Nervous	21
Overdose/Crane	22
Polyamory	23
Polyglot	24
Protection	25

Proteus	26
Purity	27
Star Eater	28
Stochastic	29
Supernal	30
Swirl/Barometer	31
Switchback	32
Tbilisi Loves You	33
Timid	34
Tin	35
Tit/Elation	36
Touch	37
Tyrannical	38
Universal	39
Wax	40
Xenomorphic	41
Zoological/Tarot	42
About the Author	43

Introduction

This book is an experiment.

I am a writer by necessity and a poet (to the extent I can claim to be one) by curiosity. As far as I know, the structure of these poems is unique. Rather than analyze this rhyme/syllable arrangement in detail, I have chosen to provide an illustrated example, with additional emphasis on the *A* lines.

All poems in this collection follow the same pattern.

Polyamory

Amorous, **generous**!	6	A
Share in Philly's gifts—cheese steak, Turkish delight	11	B
We (the **kinless**) *make*	5	A (-1 WORD)
No demands for kosher pabulum	9	C
Residue/scum remains	6	C (-1 WORD)
Of furnace-fed towns—particulates—*cake* <u>our</u>	11	A (-1 WORD)
Boots. Trudge bright/eager	5	B (-1 WORD)
Over this bulldozed flat/<u>dour</u> **landscape**	9	A (-1 WORD)

Here everything is slate/slated for a rebuild to
    Impeccable/theoretical/Stalin-strong criteria.

Last vestiges! ***Scrape*** <u>*clean*</u>	6	A (-1 WORD)
Tribe/clan/kith—primeval bond-chains, emotion	11	C (-1 WORD)
Too <u>*mean*</u>, ignoble	5	A (-1 WORD)
But for meager trivialities	9	B (-1 WORD)

The world would hum in fifths and thirds, and your boundless
    Polyamory might prove less sadistic.

I have not restricted myself to perfect end rhymes, and the imperfect rhymes (near-rhymes) I use are occasionally dependent upon unusual or unconventional pronunciations. Despite these limitations, this text constitutes my best effort to produce compositions that are more appealing than annoying.

I hope you find them worth your time.

Abandon

The mortgage was foreclosed
    By way of rational strategy—Home, say
Rock-nosed realists
    Is fungible place/parcel to be

Transacted, one key like
    All. (Float plot to plot.) Theory-locusts guess
Optimal stay time
    And returns, distress mollycoddled/

Sentimental saps, fed fabled pasts/halcyon contrivances
    From a Dune of mind-kill and organometals.

A cudgeled conformer
    Offers thanks for the beatings. Every strike, French-
Kisser sustenance/
    Blood candy/torn lips/quicklime searing

Look upon that place (never yours) as upright cordwood

    And laugh with absolute abandon.

Ad Hoc/Tethers

Your dreams have cracks built-in
    They blossom eccentrically, exploiting
Pressed-thin vagaries
    Warped ambitions, and the rolled-out breadth

Of the hundredth/millionth/
    Genius to know all/nothing, mysteries of
The True beating hard
    At your ill-tempered, glassy love for

Humankind—leaden and crystal-cut, soft
    Leaching stupefaction.

Small/solid things floor-bounce
    Large ones shatter. Ad hoc labyrinth patterns
Renounce singular
    Assembly, each sharp shard aligning

With its peers as it sees fit. All keep fractal memories of what

    You dreamt. And that tethers them to you.

Bondage/Neuroleptic

Tribes drive frenzy/tremors
    Belonging-need, an electrostatic pill
(Ignore neighbors' thoughts
    Put away this childish *want*, man) that

(Hypertoxic) rat-squeaks
    Purpose down to mere compliance, knots stomach
Torque-rends will. Nascent
    Skull-child dies in the crib, its luck run

Out when disemboweled by the ghosts of anticipated
    Disapproval (the abdomen bladed through).

Bondage is less fun than
    One might imagine if the dungeon reeks of
Desperate man and
    His quiver-sad/weep-wet penchant for

High school popularity and the adoration of crowds

    This persistent crazy warrants a neuroleptic.

Coercion

Assemblages of crap
    Prayer and chance held together—limp along
Pieces (scrap, salvaged
    Waterlogged, and septic-tank stinking)

A halfwit, thinking you
    Can multiply the sum of your damaged parts
Through will, prolong this
    March of crofters and dogcarts loaded

With gloss-glazed, perishable fortunes. (Such ego!
    Never matter, ferrous edges will sing/slice you down.)

Rot and sick, bloated from
    Prodding (and back-break labor), we accrue our
Little crumbs, scatter
    Them behind. Mice (hiss insensitive)

Will eat the better part. Raise spindly arms. Scratch your

    Name into a trunk. (This body moves but by coercion.)

Context

Fishnet of salacious
    Intent, with the loyalty one expects of
An ageless siren
    Poured into her dress, still drawing eyes

Barflies' propositions
    And the furtive/furious bodkin glances
Cast by love-denied
    Patrons, those with blotched blouses, souring

Visages, and well tequila in their cups—caustic stuff
    That eats up and etches the aluminum.

The glowering sages
    Distrust unflawed aesthetics/transmissions that
Seem of stages or
    Are crafted, made to play to pride/fools'

Rage/affection. Even I (old, emptyheaded) put no stock in

    Her/her algorithmic phrasings (regardless of context).

Damming*

Flow river, despise us
    Make mockery of our constructions, break this
State/art, *Callous Ass*
    Who demands his black-haired bride and raft

To soothe his silt-draft hate
    And moods that shift in course/direction/mass with
Their fickle kiss of
    Green and swimming life—these myth blessings

That ancient kings knew were naught but toil and vanity
    Under the golden sun.

We seek revenge. Wings spread
    Hardest hammer-forged marvels, our great contempt
Pours monsoons' dread down
    From well-earned altitudes above your

Sorry plains. We do not own you yet, but sure enough

    We will dam you.

for Hebo and his river

Decadence

Saints win by good measure
    And martyrs, too, burn through fog of decadence
Forsake pleasure, fill
    With anti-joy the hollow carcass

Of filthy Bacchus cults
    Wipe clean; sand, abrade, and polish; make still thine
Earth, your cadence-call
    Moves love-drug eunuchs to enshrine thee

But solely by your edict. Powder-formed and pressed
    Tantalum monuments endure purgatory.

Man, holy Yggdrasil
    Supplanted by a finer ash—results of
The flames still ripping
    Through woods and scrub to sprawl horizon

Watching from afar, I goggle (mute)

    At the cost of purity.

Demon Core

Repulse the fool closer—
    Berserker heart, unbeaten, wanting but space
Chance knows her quarry
    This siren song is for but the few

Pork rind flesh, new screaming—
    Depravity of expense, gory shadows
With life we grace this
    Empire of dreams(,) shot, arrows quickened

To the edge of a cadmium sky
    Where nothing falls.

Our deadened affection
    For your pursuers betrays the teeming hordes'
Chill rejection of
    The chaos and light they miss within

But without the Demon, what are we

    But animal and filth?

Disconnect

Traverse worlds, violate
    Boundaries of the unimaginative
Exsanguinate lords
    Conquer this monstrous inheritance

For dirt, a pittance thrown
    To all subordinates and wards, misfortuned
Like the native son
    And lonesome creature/things, attuned well

To the rasp of steel
    With breath.

Better the bell unheard
    From inchoate noise and pitch never grown up
No more fow/ul-bird song
    Through perpetual strife, we won peace

And we glory in the silence

    Of the disconnect.

Extra!

Pump sewage up! Up! Up!
    The tanks are empty, squealing for engorgement
Voids develop in
    Sludge but close with sufficient pressure

Back-up/bleater ruckus
    Sue for war, rally rabid sinner, sin, and
Sinless. Instant cause
    To stain the flag, to band together

Materializes where you aim chrome-plate nozzles/vituperation
    (Existential crises/anaerobic septage plead for air/ideals.)

We weather perversion
    The brownish splatter you and truck (blameless) launch
At doors (then run for
    Cover): You (instigators) pause these

Volleys, allow yourselves exit paths and ponchos, and claim

    The fecal storms and chaos were accidental/extra!

Fatigue

Decomposition starts
    With masquerade—benign maturity, grace:
Stuff time imparts to
    Those who suffered through the gauntlet, left

Scarred (but lightly), cleft/cut
    In all the correct places, true injury
Avoided—face carved
    With distinction, acne youthfulness

(And other suspect secretions) gone years ago
    Then the gilding peels.

Plaster cracks, anxious lines
    Invite fungi (and his cheerful friends)—smut/rot
Sprinkle designs of
    Their own throughout. The spores are starved for

Nothing. They gnaw/spindle through fatigue, colonize what

    We thought we owned. We are none the wiser.

Film/Barriers*

Classic plastic substrate
    Decays in passing hours. It grows eager to
Annihilate the
    Basement, pump drop-dead gas through pipes, halls

And the storied sprawl of
    The Clinic, knocking down the would-be jumpers
Even you, devout
    White-capped nurse—in these high chambers no

More hospitable than those with jelly-sealed windows—
    Will collapse, turn patina green.

New films, not so hateful
    More stretch/warp than blast, offer dove protection
They, filled and full by
    Fulsome industry—every route paved

With its good intentions—would shield us from peril—form

    Melty bubble-barriers around all (and sundry) things.

in memory of the victims of the Cleveland Clinic fire of 1929

Flavors

Polina's pussy tastes
    Like mints, the spray says. Warned, such malodorous
Below-the-waists I
    Strike from the menu (I loathe menthol)

Soldier-cabbie, haul me
    And a few bags to my (just-found) home; cry, scrape
And fuss underneath
    Attesting to the moonscape asphalt

Speak, warrior, of the scant rewards you got for a decade
    Ducking lead in the phosphorescent night.

Tyrants all assault our
    Senses—to leave us numb (blankly overwhelmed)—
To near devour one's
    Talent to know sword and sheath apart

Lies, damned lies, and their psycho-synthetic flavors

    All leave a poison aftertaste.

Genius

The weak beasts, favored by
    None: Amongst themselves, all howled calamity
(Days pass, tears dry soon)
    Another failure reduced to bone

Or in some stone encased
    Waiting for air, brisk, the rush of new moon light
Miner, pity me
    Liberate my fur/form, bright spirit

Cut away the while with bronze
    Tools fabricated by your intellect.

Follow the *bigot beast*
    Your Commander. Watch dumb as it lays waste to
Those who least comply
    Or make their life plea, insufficient

Weak beasts—you of the well-stroked ears—I wonder

    Who is the greater genius?

Hitchcock

Broken eggs hatch even
    When they shouldn't—proof of modern science and
Mercy. Ashen-faced
    Toilers, turners of worlds, save tiny

Chicks. Arbitrary heat
    In the breasts of rational men, based upon
Monkey-band instinct
    Tells friend from food (brains not brawn enough

To muscle out impulse, to scrape the slag away
    To leave pure metal).

Birds get tough, behemoth
    The ugly grows awful in them. They eat what
They can. Mammoth rage
    Godzilla-looms over extinct towns—

Payback for making feebleness suffer life—flame recompense

    For our dear compassion?

Kanagawa

From miles out, assigned this
    Shore by gravitation and high bodies (their
Chance malice opaque
    If it be more than illusory)

They crest, drown bawdy song
    Snap twain joy of vulgar innocence, break the
Oars midair, torment
    Confused/drenched men, shark and sea drawing

Close. Chump/heroes consumed by silver froth, missed only
    For their catch and jangly coin, are soon forgotten.

We are bashing brutal
    Against our liquid wall of right/wrong constructs
Briny bestial peers—
    Of salty disposition—vent spleen

Adjust and calibrate your swim bladder, prepare

    Beat and batter—in waves we suffer, you no less than I.

Legs

Glow kleptomaniacs
    Amber/pale at the boundary, moon ascends
Murk attacks eastern
    Horizon. We are all the same hue

Suspect, true outsiders
    Behind us, the maw engulfs. The nocturne for
Thieves defends nothing
    Still, we recite it to restore and

Reform our Wood's metal spines—fast-cast and
    Fragile—this, all the strength we have.

Victory, her hand sly
    Favors neither brave nor good, but the blurs of
Motion, lie given
    To promise, and the hollow ring that

Calls to Honor (that deconstructed concept

    We bandits dragged off by its legs).

Lingua Franca

Glide-tongue apparition
    Laminar over Babel/persuade-conquer
Slick addition, points
    Solid/financial justify your

Study. Dare cure baffle/
    Befuddlement. (Fail.) The Word anoints speeches
And speaker. Hubris—
    Fine, fragrant oil—leaches coherence

From utterances, transmogrifies the simple into prose-torture
    Scythe and sickle blade down/scar fewer brains than you.

The vengeance idioms
    Extract is incalculable, excessive
Story-phantoms haunt
    Harass, spook, and bully, aimless but

For their desire to catch our eyes, prick our ears, and remind

    Us that they are not so nearly dead.

Magnanimity/Unusual

In Pennsylvania's cage
    Imitation monks, penitent and hooded
Wage solitary
    Battle against moments drawn out for

Score uncalculated/
    Bone-chill centuries, entombed in crumbly hub
And spoke. Blighted beams
    Of radiance, scrub immaculate

The villainous, the libertine, the unconventionally/
    Inconveniently sadistic with a wire-bristle devotion.

Lashes taste chestnut rich
    To hunger's slender wards. They, elated by
Ghosts of smell, twitch, twirl
    And tremble. A depraved regime's fierce

Rule mandates quake-submission. Philanthropists will never

    Ask if this upright magnanimity seems a touch unusual.

Nausea

Hack up sin, ancient one
    Sputum-cough your souls—pus/ego/eternal
Indulgence. None but
    These shall survive singularity

Ton-time, which curtly called
    To oblivion's dense unity slut gluts/
Numbskull surpluses—
    These drove the market nuts, distorting

Economies/minds (yours, if not others) irreparably: Antimony-
    powdered eyes cataract from your incandescent stupid.

You are ambling about
    Flattening the mortal coil, your forestalled end
Pushed out another
    Day/mile/parsec/minute. Buses to

Heaven/hell/stops between don't venture there. Thought of

    Your never-ending nowhere trip strikes me with nausea.

Optic/Fiber/Nervous

Intersect of shock feels
    Constructions of light and genius pulse beneath
Rock, water, wheels, a
    Vast—expanse of marshes, rivers, lakes—

Wasteland. Outlaws' aches raw
    Their phlegm thickening, they dare pull away from
The monster's teeth of
    Passion, uninhibited, dumb hate

That no copper could arrest, or but much slow
    With all the lines unspooled.

We are fiber, straight and
    Without skin, unarmored, bound to law against
Planting in sand-soil
    And glass more than a Pavlov trigger

Why does this torrent of massless things

    Make us so very nervous?

Overdose/Crane

One leg, stands tall, somehow
    Forgot the other. (Good for you! It's missing)
Wings out, wow tourists
    (Fat pricks can't trundle to dinner carts

Unaided. *Sharts* collect
    In their yoga pants.) These harvests, abundant
Boosting consumption
    Make overdoses easy, stunt growth

Of anything but guts. The watchers have yet to lose a limb
    (Your Nitinol-tough frame was not as fortunate.)

I am loath/disinclined
    To figure you the wiser. (Select martyr's
Credits.) Blind, prideful
    You, untended on the barren beach

Hurt no less than the roly-poly abhorrence double fisting

    Crisco sticks (and he wants only for a coronary).

Polyamory

Amorous, generous!
    Share in Philly's gifts—cheese steak, Turkish delight
We (the kinless) make
    No demands for kosher pabulum

Residue/scum remains
    Of furnace-fed towns—particulates—cake our
Boots. Trudge bright/eager
    Over this bulldozed flat/dour landscape

Here everything is slate/slated for a rebuild to
    Impeccable/theoretical/Stalin-strong criteria.

Last vestiges! Scrape clean
    Tribe/clan/kith—primeval bond-chains, emotion
Too mean, ignoble
    But for meager trivialities

The world would hum in fifths and thirds, and your boundless

    Polyamory might prove less sadistic.

Polyglot

Sclerotic/necrotic/
    Phonologically malfeasant, my tongue/
Brain, narcotic slow
    From drug-terrible age, butchers the

Syllables. Crash sea sounds—
    Where words/more than shriek chaos/low-low grumbles
Should be—among few
    Bulb-pop recalls, naught else stumbles up

On legs, tetanus crushed, box pressed with nickel-star cigars
    What survives the bear trap snap is mangled permanent.

Meaning dies, syrup of
    Incomprehensibility coats, rounds down
Points, foxglove-fingers
    Malfunctioning chests, lets you convey

Agonized ambiguity (if you struggle long/noble). I am expert

    At this, this torture (for I was never much of a polyglot).

Protection

SHRIEK/SHRIEK (BABY) SHRIEK/SHRIEK
    Drowning! Too late the tattler (to save the girls)
Phobic-weak, fearful
    No virility, servility

Doughboy-chunky meekness
    So enraptured by shrew-daemon/cackle-beasts
He hurls violence
    Harsh verbiage, and grovel-feasts on

Damsel/adulteress disdain. Shiny armor, bastard sword
    Anchor man to muck. (He can't protect anyone.)

Think lust scarce, pawn yourself
    Shortages are summoned, conjured bleakness to
Relegate shelf-stored
    Seconds to chaste-brisk silence, wastelands

Where seed falls (if it does at all) on grit logged with

    Fluids of questionable provenience and composition.

Proteus*

Catch the liquid lapping
    Heavy in the dark, formless, evasive, and
All foretelling, to
    Strong-hand kings and clever Electric

Generals, slick-witted
    Practical and brilliant, seeing virtue in
Grand monstrosities
    Waves, laggard memory, and djinn tricks

In the glacial flare of mercury and arc, I shift and bend
    A bloodless, barren, passing shadow.

Night burns guards who fix gaze
    Long at fragile glass and blasted violet
These blaze aplenty
    Give nil for discernment and bees' stings

Was this excessive, unnecessary

    For a globe repoured according to your will?

*for Charles Proteus Steinmetz

Purity

Unadulterated
    Horizon, stretch blue-bowl dimensions from ground-
Weighted boundary
    To deep-diffuse and cloudless zenith

Sturdy trilith pillars—
    Cathedral of elements/purity—hold
Up. Surround decay
    And abandonment fold together

All the venerable beliefs. But none are quite as thin
    As the goldsmith-beaten sky.

Dome is feather-heavy
    Soap bubbles, wax, tallow, scent—the chandler's wares
In beefy portions
    Could cleanse all, leaving only bay rum

Redolence (and well-starched propriety). And down the drain

    We'd go.

Star Eater

And the Old One broke through
    Defeating the last of the great ordinals
Tear these too, swallow—
    He leaves but void, no temperature

Greedy wail, impure want—
    Frost extends from his gut, up, down low, outwards
Darkness nulls vision
    But he can see what dreams and words will

To power, unalloyed
    (We are not in them.)

Oh God of Ill Spirit
    Who confined the One? Why with such gaunt machines?
None can outwit All
    Yet you stood till our collision came

Now you grow warm with fury

    Readying for what?

Stochastic

Unencumbered rambles
    Logic of expedient locomotion—
He mangles orders
    Of monochronic rationalists

The goal? That gusts' guidance
    Will show him the Way, time's stone-faced hoarders be
Damned. The notion of
    Perfect prediction, a tree growing

Up and true (platonic thing), is orgasmic fantasy for dead-soul
    Dullards (and killjoys with pot metal fangs).

There are cliffs calling out
    But softly. Fair winds follow hills, nuisance bluffs
No knockabout's fear
    (They choose air carefully: It shoves them

Towards the sun, the satellites, the interstellar speckle—

    The glory w/he'd otherwise miss.)

Supernal

Higher minds than mine, more
    August, have ascended to make oblate round
To fix the score, bad
    May it be, with methods more boggling

To them we cling, panic
    Terror, the ice December of our mad hearts
Ringers sound alarms
    June bugs and curs scatter to parts known

Well by zamak men, easily liquefied
    And their yellow-bellied friends (and fellow travelers).

Pummel us, risks blown out
    Of proportion. March us towards manic doom
We shall doubt nothing
    April shower dread/drizzle charms us

After the flood, we hope for diamond skies

    And an orb smooth-clean.

Swirl/Barometer*

Dry wood has potential
    Calories (greatness) dance in the cellulose
Blissful faeries
    (Spark-ball rascals) have but to let them

Loose. Smear dim atmosphere
    With frightful radiance. Canaries chorused
Warnings (for close care)
    But the carnival—felled forest now

Felled again at center—is no/t mine: It's more dangerous
    Glee swirls up with the rust-nail crumble.

Creation's joys wow less
    Effectively than destruction's cashmere-wrap
Comforts caress those
    Who stand outside, work and wear having

Turned their hides to leather (or coated them with fog-filth

    Resignation). (The crowd's eyes are a certain barometer.)

for J.M.W. Turner's "The Burning of the Houses of Lords and Commons"

Switchback

Truth sets free those too poor
    To buy a decent lie, but for non-losers—
(Us) those with more than
    Chump change and fool notions—*pravda* binds/

Liberates, blinds/bestows
    Vision as power, payment, and plan dictate
Tramps, users (hungry
    For unsavory flavors) plate lick

Last morsels of cock and crow stew, sing fine as the birds
    They *et*, and dull their flatware across the china.

Hill of spotted dick (up
    From treacle and sticky-slip plains) arose to
Wallop merciless
    Appetites and boozy intestines

Slow absorption of the poison ingested, prolong the last meal

    Switchback to the summit and confuse everyone.

Tbilisi Loves You

Pauper mutt, forever
    Proud (vigilant and wary), keep ears up, eyes
Open, never turn
    Back on friends, enemies, or strangers

You and yours—forebears and
    Peers, none too easily excited—yearn not
To know. Wise even
    As pups, you saw what brilliance wrought, man's

Peculiar and varied ways, coming from all corners
    As though magnets, pushed/pulled by poles.

Roads crumble, plans resume—
    Silk, spice, the orient's artistry, sand—the
Mountains bloom, prosper
    Trek and trekkers bring peace, flatten (or

Smooth over a little) our differences, and a dog's hair's

    Worth of brandy soothes beast and man alike.

Timid

Palpitations thumping
    Adrenal-jolt vision, pupils pinhead tight
Star points twinkling gray
    Eat the periphery, steal language

Wrong move—carnage, misted
    Pink. My foot presses down a switch. I pray the
Blaze-red pain might stop
    So us lot—you, me, he—*we*—expire

If at all, as heroes. Swing brass censers round in tribute
    Slaughter asthmatics with dragon's blood.

Temple-fire spindle
    Bathe lacunae in photons and twisted smoke
Give ample jaundice
    To angels, ecstatic, atop white

Sepulchers. All would be thus honored

    Were I not so timid.

Tin

Acid strips the body
    Leaving bones—blanched scaffolding, a rictus, scrap—
Spotless/spotty, no
    Recollection of the shock-sizzle

That gnawed through banal breath
    Moves obliterate everything—I throw out
The crap, unopened
    Gently used with the same stout firmness

Strong corrosives, conflagrations to melt a tungsten crucible—
    These dare not take as much as necessity and water.

Smoke (formless) obfuscates
    But gently, reversibly, with breadth greater
Than depth—Puffs, gates to
    . . . something, some wisdom, not bargained for

Not earned, close off a citadel of dust memory

    As I torch/ember through my last tin of tobacco.

Tit/Elation

Scream psychotic over
    Purity. Feign, faint, and swoon. You, undefiled
Purr scurrilously
    Pale ankles, maimed faces, lusterless

Stare—Wound-atlas engraved
    Into rose flesh. (Fume bughouse mad.) Busty blondes
Are sacred. Mild man
    (Kind he claims to be) responds, reacts

Rebar erect in his recliner, to this horror of horrors—loss of a
    Beautiful soul—but the channel doesn't change.

Our icon distracts us
    From vexatious shuffle down shit-paved alleys
With bodice-ripping
    Tales of lust-evil—the plan: malice

Aforethought and canned-gasp revulsion made addictive

    Beneath the goodness/veneer, there are tits/gore/elation.

Touch*

Not knowing where they moved
    The Temple, I roam drunk-quick under clouds of
Unproved novelty
    Tracks of man and thinking beasts fading

In high-bog, cladding damp—
    Sap strength, dissolve it. Soil acidity, green
Pines keep above ground
    Sterile (or almost), a clean surface—

That delights with fragrance, torments with touch
    And razorblades in two the united senses.

Sand grabs feet. Nervous streams
    Whisper past the thirsty muck as sky (lamp)black
Pulls sun and dreams down
    To dusk. Hearing dragon and hound draw

Near, I hide in an empty ditch and hope neither they

    Nor earth and root consume me with passion.

*with respect to Wang Wei's "On the Way to the Temple"

Tyrannical

Tessellated truth was
    Always illusory. We cannot foresee
When horror draws near
    Glory, too, comes with little warning

We (unblind, morning rays
    Casting in hues of infrared and fear our
Frames) barely risen
    Know that the tiles devour everything

Every possibility, subject to action at a distance
    Non-repetition, the iron law.

Pen and rose, we bring no
    Other weapons (but this faintest of praise for
Slipping flow devoid
    Of friction). The bubbling basin that

Never exhausts

    Warns us in rhyme and chance.

Universal

Orange-coal radiant
    With a microfine ash as insulation
Resplendent goodwill
    Melt-sinks into practitioners like

A hot knife through pike fat
    (Here the fishiness is endless—an ill reek
Raising passion and
    Nausea enough to peak roguish

Surges in my anguished gut [companion/frustration/
    Frail abomination/fulminate-bang truth detector].)

Goatish dispositions
    (In skins of lion/lamb gentle strength that no
Man's volitions could
    Wear as one) raise their horny band from

Troughs of passing moments/a suspect soup/hot salt kettles

    Hate and romance scams are universal.

Wax

Hubris of impression—
    Anti-empirical/primal energy
Deft transgression of
    Normative rules of Manichaean

Nay, Galilean warp
    And woof. (You know these incantations, suave boss
And how to free less
    Privileged empire subjects. Gloss smooth

Over your skepticism [worth less than a pewter button] for
    We/you/thy/thee have bills to pay.)

Deconstruct and move those
    Conjoined tyrannies of law/order. Harp on
What prose platitudes
    Resonate tonewood heads/stress raw

Nerves. Vibrate anything enough with noise and watch

    It puddle. Reduce the seal to wax/blob Rorschach.

Xenomorphic

Impress upon the grains
    How very small they are (odd and out of place)
Pressure strains structures
    Exacts a toll on nonconforming

Arrangements, warming as
    It, scornful of wisp electrons, alters their
Space/energetic
    Architectures. Bare limitations

For self-guided growth manifest when eons' platinum
    Hands squeeze with a noble, pathological unconcern.

Locations, mutations
    Of geography (the un/shaking jazz drift
Peoples/nations, s/oil
    Experience), mimetic tribal

Substitutes—these (briefly) fascinate me when I pass them

    By (but never longer). (My shape is slightly different.)

Zoological/Tarot

Monochrome in lunar
    Flare. The Roman trail to the vanishing point
Is leaf-quiver hushed
    Wolves pad behind, nosy/peckish, glint

Of disciplined flint-spin
    Heat evident and able to combust/char
Down joint invention
    Of void-pitch and deep quasar twinkle

We will outrun the dusk, determined to conceal ourselves
    Before scornful day paints cobalt blue over mystery.

Men—the booze-barrel waft
    From pores and yap-yap word-holes (kith/kin along
For kicks, aloft horse
    Or peasant) foul—think us common game

(And not much more), will hunt us as wild packs would deem

    Unsportsmanlike. (There is nothing good in the cards.)

About the Author

Brant von Goble is a writer, editor, publisher, researcher, teacher, musician, juggler, and amateur radio operator.

He received a Doctor of Education degree from Western Kentucky University in 2017. During his doctoral studies, he researched the impact of motivational training on the social and emotional development of students.

www.ingramcontent.com/pod-product-compliance
Lightning Source LLC
Chambersburg PA
CBHW050324010526
44119CB00003B/94